Abba, Father, Daddy

Ava Matthews

Illustrator: Eric Austin

Archway Publishing books may be ordered through booksellers or by contacting:

Archway Publishing
1663 Liberty Drive
Bloomington, IN 47403
www.archwaypublishing.com
1 (888) 242-5904

Because of the dynamic nature of the Internet, any web addresses or links contained in this book may have changed since publication and may no longer be valid. The views expressed in this work are solely those of the author and do not necessarily reflect the views of the publisher, and the publisher hereby disclaims any responsibility for them.

Any people depicted in stock imagery provided by Thinkstock are models, and such images are being used for illustrative purposes only.
Certain stock imagery © Thinkstock.

ISBN: 978-1-4808-2114-9 (sc)
ISBN: 978-1-4808-2115-6 (e)

Print information available on the last page.

Archway Publishing rev. date: 04/11/2022

Proverbs 22:6
Train up a child in the way he
should go: and when he is old,
he will not depart from him it.

Mommy, where is my daddy?

Jr., we discussed this before, your daddy had to go away for awhile. Unfortunately, he is not going to be in your life for a few years. He wants you to know that he loves you, Jr., and that he will be writing you. When he returns, you two will be together again.

I am here for you sweetie, and I love you too!

And, did you know that God loves you as well, and he lives in your heart and is here for you too?

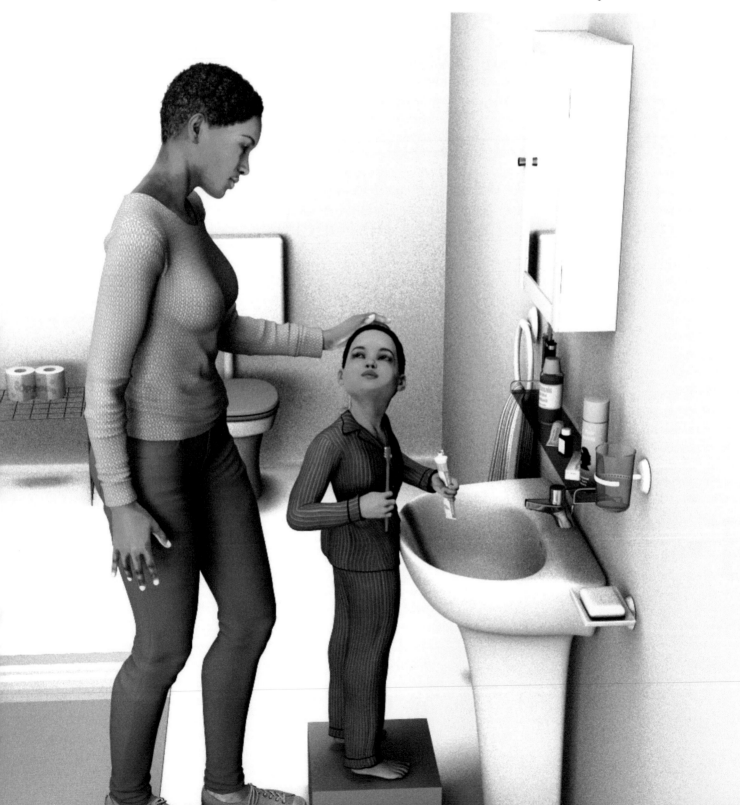

Uh, huh.

God wants to be as close to you as your dad, Jr., if you will let him. He wants to be your Abba, Father or Daddy.

What does Abba Father mean mom?

It means your heavenly Father.

How can God be my father if I can't see him or hear him?

You can't see the wind can you?

No!

But, you know that the wind is there and it is everywhere, right?

Yeh.

Well, it's the same with God. He is everywhere but, unlike the wind he even lives in you and speaks to your heart.

Wow! Really!

Mom, I never heard him speak.
How can I hear him speak to me?
Does he sound like the wind?

No, Jr., he doesn't sound like the wind when he speaks. God speaks to you in many different ways. He speaks to you through the Bible stories that I read to you. He speaks to you through prayer, and he speaks to you through adults who give you direction in life. These are just a few ways that he speaks to you.

You know, there was a young boy in the Bible in a similar situation like yours. His name was Samuel. Samuel did not have his earthly mom or dad in his life, and he had to learn to depend upon God as his Abba, Father, Daddy.

Samuel went on to become one of the most important ministers in his day and in the Bible.

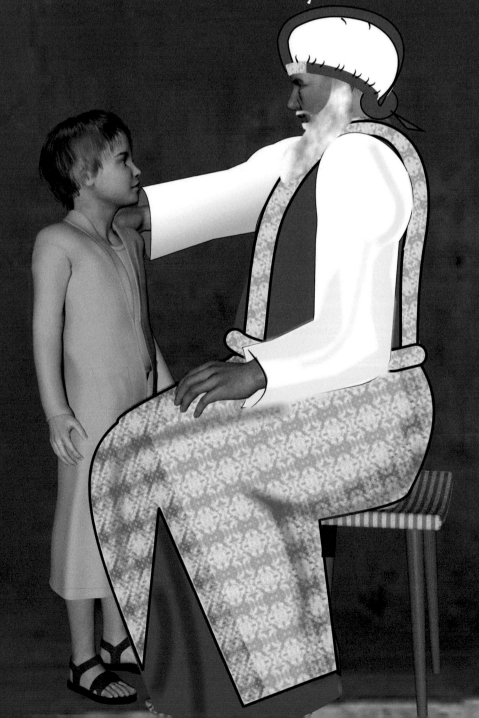

Samuel learned to pray to God and hear what God was saying to him.

Your heavenly Father can become as real to you as your earthly father. He loves you, Jr., and he gets excited every time you pray to him. He wants you learn to depend on him even more than you depend on your earthly father.

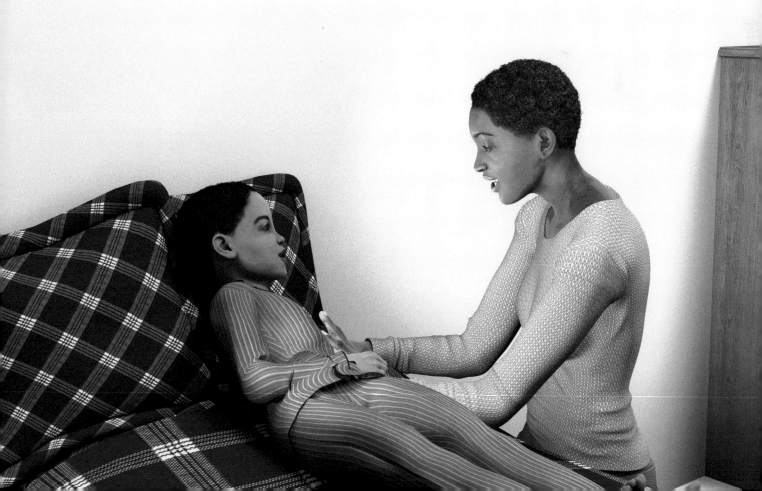

How do I get to know him better, mom?

You can start by praying to him, like you were taught in Sunday school. Then, start looking for the answer to your prayers. You know he has answered you when your prayers are answered.

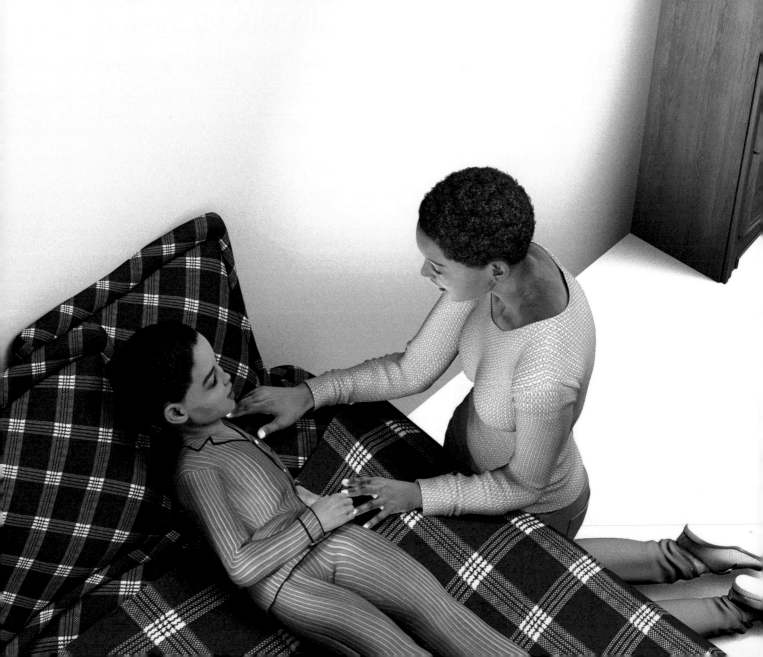

You get to know him better by letting me and others read the Bible stories to you and then discuss the stories with those who read the stories to you.

At any rate, Jr., God knows you need a man in your life right now who can help you mature into manhood. No one can replace your dad, but God wants you to have a man in your life that can help point you to him. That is why I have asked one of the men at church to help mentor you while dad is away.

The little boy in the Bible, Samuel, had a mentor to help him too. His name was Eli. Eli did not replace Samuel's dad in his life, but he helped Samuel mature as a man and helped point Samuel to God and to get to know him as his Abba, Father, Daddy.

What is a mentor mom?

A mentor is someone who helps you grow up son. He will talk with you about man things and more than likely, you will go to different fun places together.

OK mommy, I think I want a mentor.

Good, now say your prayers and go to sleep, because we have a busy day tomorrow.

OK mom. And I am going to pray for Abba, Father, Daddy to send my dad home to me soon.

God, thank you for being my
Abba, Father, Daddy too!